Compete Or Die!

By

Mark Reinsberg

Compete Or Die!
by Mark Reinsberg

Copyright © 2023

All Rights reserved.

No part of this publication may be reproduced, stored in a retrieval system, or transmitted in any form or by any means, electronic, mechanical, photocopying or Otherwise, without the written permission of the publisher.
The author/editor asserts the moral right to be identified as the author/editor of this work.

ISBN: 978-93-59955-63-6
Published by

DOUBLE 9 BOOKS

2/13-B, Ansari Road
Daryaganj, New Delhi – 110002
info@double9books.com
www.double9books.com
Tel. 011-40042856

ABOUT THE AUTHOR

"Compete or Die!" with the aid of Mark Reinsberg stands as a literary masterpiece, a testament to the author's brilliance in forging a profound connection between the geographical regions of commercial enterprise and leadership. With a dedicated attempt to illuminate the problematic dynamics of those domain names, Reinsberg's work becomes a guiding beacon for readers, fostering a deeper expertise and connection among individuals navigating the complexities of expert life. Reinsberg's writing transcends mere instruction; it's far a creative and passionate exploration of various regions and emotions within the enterprise panorama. Through his narratives, readers aren't most effective exposed to the pragmatic elements of opposition however are also invited to resonate with the human stories woven into the material of management and entrepreneurship. Elegance defines Reinsberg's prose, making the complexities of enterprise and leadership handy to a large target audience. His wonderful testimonies unfold with a seamless mixture of sophistication and simplicity, making sure that every reader, regardless of background, can revel in the splendor of his insights. Mark Reinsberg emerges now not just as an author but as a storyteller who no longer best imparts know-how however also cultivates a fun literary revel in. "Compete or Die!" is a manifestation of his dedication to facilitating connections and enriching understanding, making it an imperative read for those navigating the intricacies of the professional global.

I slammed the aircar door and fumbled in my pocket for the key. I cast a quick backward glance at the policeman a hundred feet away.

He wheeled about at the sound.

My trembling fingers tried to fit the key into the ignition.

"Halt!" the policeman yelled unlimbering his gun and breaking into a run.

My fingers failed to coordinate. I heard a shot and nervously dropped the key. I bent over frantically to scoop it up.

There was another shot. Pieces of glass trickled down my neck. I straightened up and saw a hole in the windshield, level with my eyes.

"Hands up!" The cop had slowed down to take careful aim. He was so close now he could hardly miss.

"Don't shoot!" I shouted. "I surrender!"

I inserted the key in the ignition with desperate precision, gunning the engines so hard that the ship spun halfway around. The policeman leaped out of the way as my Cad Super roared past him and lurched into the air.

I heard a tattoo of shots from the ground and then we were out of range.

I swore as the acceleration crushed me deep into the seat. My forehead was pounding.

"Bart Sponsor, fugitive," I thought bitterly. "And only a half-hour ago I was a pillar of society. Worst thing I had to worry about was a speeding ticket...."

... I had been griping to my wife as usual about the rush-hour morning traffic above Chicago.

"Look at this. Just look at this," I said disgustedly.

Below us, the lanes were choked with ponderous, slow-moving commuter copters. Around us, flivver-jets clogged the expressway like millions of migrating birds. We couldn't make more than three hundred miles an hour.

"The stupid shlubs," I muttered resentfully. "They ought to ride the pneumatic tubes to work."

"The airlanes should be reserved for Top Competitors only," said Celia teasingly. "Like you, dear."

I ignored her sarcasm and scanned the empty lane overhead. All that blue sky set aside for outgoing traffic, and nothing in sight. A shameful waste.

I gunned our Cad Super, joyfully, defiantly, and scooted up over the assigned traffic stream at a thousand per. Celia gave me an alarmed look.

"Bart! You'll get a ticket."

I grinned and kicked our speed up an additional two hundred.

Illegal, of course, but I made terrific time crossing the Iowa-Illinois border where Chicagoland begins. I didn't squeeze back into the expressway until mighty Municipal Tower came into view through the dense industrial haze above Lake Michigan. There atop the building stood a gigantic sign revolving on a pivot with the wind. It bore the seal of Chicago and the stunning legend: I WILL COMPETE. Most inspiring motto in the world, I think.

Celia touched my hand. "We'll have to stop at the bank first."

"No time," I said. "We're due at the school at nine-thirty."

"It won't hurt to be a few minutes late. This is important, Bart."

We have a good marriage, and I don't quarrel with Celia's wishes. But this meant another delay, and I could already see half the morning shot, what with the meeting in the principal's office, and afterwards perhaps taking Freddie out for a soda or something to make him feel secure and loved. What a lot of trouble that boy was getting into lately.

I wheeled out of traffic and feathered down to the roof of the 1st National. A conveyer belt carried our ship toward the teller's window.

Celia opened her purse and withdrew a bank form. "Here, I think you'll have to sign this, darling."

I voiced my irritation. "Withdraw it in your own name. It's a joint account. Personally, I don't understand how you can need more money when I just gave you four hundred yesterday."

"This is a very large amount," said Celia softly. "Bank requires it."

"How much?" I asked suspiciously.

"Ten thousand." She was staring at me intently with her almond-shaded eyes. Her full red lips were parted in the faintest trace of a smile, as her neat brown-pencilled eyebrows arched slightly in amused defiance.

She was daring me to ask the obvious question. Hell, I thought, I can afford it. I signed the form and passed it back to her.

We were at the teller window. She scribbled on the sheet and handed it to the clerk.

"Now," I said, feeling that I'd fulfilled the code of gallantry, "may I ask what you need it for?"

"Certainly, dear. I'm giving it to the Mendelsohns as a going-away present. Tonight at their farewell party."

"What! Ten thousand credits? Are you insane! The Mendelsohns mean nothing to me." I was so upset that I kicked the degravity pedal and we started to rise from the roof. I brought us down with a thud.

"They mean a lot to me," said Celia calmly. "They used to mean a lot to you too."

"But ten thousand!" I protested. "What do you think I am, a millionaire philanthropist?"

"It is a lot of money," Celia agreed placatingly. "But the Mendelsohns are leaving tomorrow for Primus Gladus. We'll never see them again."

"So what!" I said heatedly. "Thousands of people go to the stars as colonists. Thousands of failures like the Mendelsohns think their luck will change on another planet. Does this mean that—"

"Bart, consider," said Celia. "If they had remained here on Earth as our friends, there would have been many occasions in a lifetime when I would have sent them remembrances. The birth of children. Anniversaries. Graduations. Confirmations, bar mitzvahs, wedding presents. Funeral wreaths. All I've done now is roll up all those gifts of a lifetime into one farewell present, of a size that will help them a little on their new world."

"I've cut off a lot of heads for that money. Grain brokerage is a brutal profession, what with thirty billion mouths clamoring for food, and the government keeping speculation in a straight-jacket, and that insurrection on Venus, the granary of the solar system, making wheat futures a nightmare. This kind of generosity leaves me cold. I had more to say on the subject, but the bank teller spoke up to Celia.

"Your identification, please?"

Celia showed him her wrist plate.

"Ah, Mrs. Sponsor, I'm sorry to inconvenience you, but this is such a large amount that we'll need your husband's personal verification. Bank rules, you know."

"This is my husband."

My irritation mounted. "I'm Sponsor," I said to the teller, flourishing my wrist band. "What's the difficulty?"

"Ah, Mr. Sponsor, would you like to step in a moment and speak to our chief cashier?"

"I haven't time," I blurted sharply. "Give my wife the money!" We were already ten minutes late to our school appointment.

The teller looked abashed and hesitant.

"Look here," I demanded, "if we don't get better service around here I'll take my account elsewhere!"

That did it. He fussed around and finally handed Celia the bundle which she had some trouble fitting into her purse. "Small denominations," she explained. I gunned our car peevishly, I must admit, and the acceleration shoved her back into the seat rest. We were ten minutes late already. I should have called my office.

We soared into air above old Chicago, the part rebuilt after World War III. The lake claimed a good share of the blast area, of course, but that's what makes our city so unusually beautiful now. Four hundred tiny islands dot the lakefront, some connected by causeways, others reachable only by aircar or boat.

"Why are you so cross?" said Celia, taking the offensive the way women do when they've pulled some outrageous stunt.

"Look, you can't have it both ways. You can give them the money, but you can't get me to say I like the idea."

"Solly Mendelsohn was once your closest friend."

"Solly is a poor competitor, Celia. Let's face up to it. He has brains. He once showed signs of being a brilliant soil chemist, but he washed out of school. And then he became a fertilizer salesman, and he couldn't make a go of that. And after that he took up hydroponic farming, but he wasn't a success at that either. No wonder he wants to try another planet!"

"Solly has had a lot of personal misfortunes."

"That's an excuse all the shlubs use. No. The fact is, he just can't compete. And unless you compete in this world, you're dead."

Below on its own crescent-shaped island lay Chicago Classical School. I put our ship into a fast elevator dive. "My sympathies," I added, "go to Dolores. She's a bright, attractive kid. Keen competitor. She didn't deserve a shlub for a husband." I paused. "And about that party they're giving tonight. I'm not going."

Chicago Classical was frankly a boarding school for privileged kids. It taught the first six years, and no better I'm sure than the public schools of Chicago. But there was social distinction. The contacts would be good for Freddie later on. Freddie boarded there five days a week and came home to us on weekends, uncommunicative about his experiences, but happy to go romping with me in the woods and ravine adjoining our estate near Mason City. Unfortunately, that wasn't too often. Competitive pressure kept me in Chicago sometimes three or four weeks at a stretch.

When they gave the first graders a word-picture test, Celia once told me, Freddie had represented the word *father* by the symbols of a bald head, pipe and briefcase. After that, whenever I couldn't get home on Saturday or Sunday, I made an effort to have lunch with the boy in Chicago at least once during the week. But of course you can't get to know your son very well that way.

"Just what is this trouble Freddie's involved in?" I asked as we descended. "Why don't you keep me better informed on the boy?"

"I try to, but when have you had time to listen? I usually see you at our cocktail parties for clients, or else at three in the morning when you drop into bed too exhausted to get into pajamas."

"Well, this matter with the principal. Are you sure it's so serious?"

"They never ask for both parents unless it is," Celia assured me, glancing soberly at the school buildings as we came to earth.

We parked, I noticed, alongside a dark blue official car, with the municipal seal, and the initials S.T.A.R.S. "Never heard of that one," I told Celia as we walked to the main dormitory and administration building.

The place was a gloomy gray, vine-covered neo-gothic structure which ignored almost a thousand years of architectural progress. An old-fashioned electric eye opened the door. Inside, the building smelled like stale bread, musty linen and floor varnish, combined with a dash of urine. The interior lighting was unnaturally bright, it seemed to me, like in a surgical arena. The only harmonious note was struck by the mural in the vestibule. One entire wall was covered by an allegorical painting of sports, professions, and industry, with the phrase COMPETE OR PERISH emblazoned boldly across the top.

Celia nudged me. "A little raw for school kids, don't you think?"

This was an old, unhealed grievance between us. "Those are the twenty-fourth century facts of life," I replied evenly.

We reported to the receptionist robot in an alcove controlling the inner set of doors.

"You are fifteen minutes late," said the machine. "I will announce you. Be seated please."

We remained standing. I spied a public wall phone and jerked into awareness. "Excuse me, honey. I have to call the office!"

I hastily dialed our number and got the busy signal. Wow! All nine lines were tied up, including our human and our robot receptionists. I immediately dialed our unlisted private number, and somebody answered with a curse, and I knew it was my partner Charlie Spacker.

"Compete, man! Compete!" he shouted. "Where the hell are you?"

"Chicago Classical School. Personal problem. I told you about it."

"Well, get over here quick! That Venus situation is about to blow up, and we're tied up to the tune of three hundred million in wheat and soybeans!"

"I'll be over within a half hour. Meanwhile, have Claire book passage on the next Venus rocket. One of us has got to go there."

"Willco," said Claire. She always monitored our calls.

"All right," stormed Charlie, "that may help us a month from now. But what about now? Do I buy or sell? These customers are drowning me!"

Charlie was a great bluff man who inspired the clients' confidence, but he quailed at policy decisions. I thought fast. I'd go there and make a deal with the insurrectionists. Help finance the rebellion in exchange for exclusive first option. If they won, good. If they lost, status quo anyway.

Celia was gesturing urgently as the inner door opened.

"Buy!" I said and I slammed down the receiver.

It was hard to adjust to the dim lighting in the principal's office. His room was loaded with antique fiberglass furniture of the twenty-first century. He sat behind, or rather within, a donut-shaped desk, a moon-faced man with short, monk-like haircut, and bulbous nose.

"You are the parents of Edmund Sponsor?" We nodded. He pressed a button. "Very well. We will send for the boy."

He swivelled around to face a wall of slanting glass which overlooked the children's playground. We could see two ranks of boys in a tug-of-war, and some little girls playing red-rover.

"Scott," he said into a tiny microphone on his desk top. A playground instructor looked up.

"Yes, sir?"

"Please send Edmund Sponsor to my office."

"He's not here, sir. I believe he's in the dormitory."

"How does that happen?" demanded the principal. "This is game time."

"He declined to join in the competition, sir."

"I see. Thank you."

I felt a hot flush of embarrassment. My son non-competitive? That seemed impossible. He must be ill. It was an insulting accusation.

The principal flicked on the wall visa-screen. It showed a lean, rather formally-attired man seated on a lounge in the anteroom, next to a uniformed policeman.

"Masefield? I believe it would expedite matters if you would find Edmund Sponsor in the dormitory and bring him here. Would you do that, please?"

Masefield nodded and the screen darkened. The principal turned to us.

"This incident on the playground which you just witnessed may perhaps spare us all an overly long explanation. Mr. Sponsor, I have been in touch with your wife from time to time, and I assume she has kept you informed on your boy's progress. Or should we say, lack of progress?"

I felt a sense of numb shock. Celia had told me nothing. I managed to control my outward signs of surprise. "Yes, she has," I said calmly, crossing my legs. "But of course we have a fiercely competitive line, and I haven't been able to follow the situation as well as one might wish.

"Would you tell me, in brief, what it all amounts to, and what you suggest as a remedy? Both Mrs. Sponsor and I are willing and eager to cooperate."

"I hope," said the principal, "that you will remember what you have just said when I propose the remedy. As to the problem itself, I must put it bluntly—your son Edmund refuses to compete."

If any other man had said this to me I would have smashed his face in. Celia looked at me warningly. Again I masked my feelings.

"This is a terrible thing to hear," I said sweetly. "But surely it can't be as stark and simple as that. Freddie must be ill or emotionally disturbed. Have your doctors given him a checkup? Have your psychoanalysts examined him?"

"Long ago and continually, Mr. Sponsor. That was your wife's original suggestion. Your boy was completely uncooperative with the analysts. Resistant. Negatively competitive, if you know what I mean. In fact, I will repeat what one of our doctors said. If your boy could reverse his attitude, and put all the energy he uses to fight the system into battling his future economic opponents, he'd become a Top Competitor. However, a year has gone by, and we have not been able to bring about the slightest change. Now, in fact, the situation has gotten out of hand."

"But," I said, trying to sound detached and clinical, "how does this non-competitiveness, as you say, manifest itself in our son?" The prefix *non* had a bitter taste in my mouth.

"In every way," said the principal. "He won't play competitive games with the other children. Intellectually, he won't exert himself against his classmates. Financially, he refuses to earn bonus points selling magazine subscriptions in his leisure time. This, as you know, goes against the very principles on which our democracy is based. It's subversive in its influence on the other children. If he were not so young, if he did not come from a well-known competitive family, one would almost be tempted to think Edmund an Australian spy!"

"Come now!" said Celia indignantly. "Expel Freddie from your school if you wish, but don't slander him."

The door buzzed softly, then slid open. Freddie entered, followed closely by Masefield.

Freddie had been crying. His eyes opened wide and an expression of joy hit his face as he saw us.

"Mother!" he exclaimed, rushing to Celia's arms. She hugged him fervently. I patted him manfully on the shoulder, but I felt shy and a little inept. "Dad!" he added, running the back of one hand across his tear-stained cheeks.

"How are you, son?" I said inadequately.

Freddie looked up at me imploringly. "Take me away from here, dad. *Please* take me away from here!" He buried his head on Celia's breast and started to sob.

"We will, darling," said Celia. We exchanged swift glances.

"We certainly will, son, if you're unhappy here," I said rather mechanically. I was, to tell the truth, rather shocked by the emotional display. Freddie had always been such a self-contained little boy, so beyond his years in control and understanding, so undemonstrative.

"I think," said the principal portentously, "that matters would be best served if Edmund waited outside."

"I agree." There was no reason for Freddie to hear whatever remained to be said.

The kid made quite a fuss about leaving us, even for a few minutes, but in the end Masefield escorted him out with friendly firmness.

"We are all in accord then, that your son is to leave Chicago Classical School?"

"I think so," said Celia, with unconcealed hostility.

"What steps do we take now?" I asked more civilly. "Do we enroll him in the second grade of public school? I mean, is his work here fully transferable?"

The principal seemed to reach very carefully for his next words. He seemed in fact faintly apprehensive. "Mr. Sponsor, under normal circumstances a child's credits from Chicago Classical are acceptable at more than par in the public school system. But this is a case in which the authorities are obliged to exercise jurisdiction."

"Just what do you mean by that?" Celia said angrily.

"Darling," I said patting her hand, "control yourself. Let's try to hear this thing objectively."

"Yes, Mrs. Sponsor, as your husband has said, this is a matter which requires considerable detachment. We two have had a number of conversations in the past year, and I must say candidly that you did not seem to realize the delicacy and seriousness of Edmund's problem. By authorities I mean, of course, the juvenile delinquency courts."

"Now I'm the one who doesn't understand," I said very mildly.

"You are aware, Mr. Sponsor, that aggressive non-competitiveness is carried on the statute books as a misdemeanor."

Scorn and ridicule were in Celia's voice. "But Freddie is a seven-year-old!"

"Quite. But our concern as educators is with the future adult. And unless the child's habits of thought are corrected in the early, formative years, all of his aberrations are magnified by maturity. Would you want your son to grow up a criminal, a seditionist?"

"You need not worry about that," I answered firmly. "I'll take Freddie in hand. He'll learn the value of competition if I have to beat it into him!"

"I'm afraid it's a little too late for that," said the educator. "School is a powerful influence, but home is the decisive influence in the molding of a child's character and outlook. The plain and simple fact is that your home—Edmund's home—has been an *anti*-competitive influence! No school can counterbalance it."

"That's absurd! Do you realize what line of business I'm engaged in?"

"I'm fully aware of that. However, how much time do you actually spend with your son, teaching him the precepts of our democracy?"

"What are you driving at?"

He had made up his mind to say it. He leaned forward across his donut-shaped desk and said very deliberately: "When the home fails in its duty, the state must step in and do the job. We have recommended that Edmund be placed in our city's Special Training and Re-Education School, and that he be isolated from all parental influence for a period of five years. Or until such time as his attitude shall have displayed a fundamental change."

Celia was on her feet. "What! You mean we can't see him for five years!"

I was leaning over his desk, almost yelling. "You are not going to take our boy away from us. We'll fight it in the courts."

The principal likewise stood up. He stared at us, disdainful in his power. "The court has already decided that point. I thought you were sensible, cooperative people who were willing to fight and sacrifice for the preservation of Competition. I thought I was doing you a special favor in giving you a last moment or two with your son. That, you must understand, went against all rules. I'm sorry now that I extended you the favor."

Celia was tearfully, bitterly sarcastic. "You extended us the favor—"

I was trembling with rage. "We are taking Freddie with us."

"You can't."

"You just try to stop me."

The principal smiled, again disdainfully. "He has already left with the STARS officer. There is nothing you can do. Except leave my office."

I was stunned. That blue car we parked next to. I was paralyzed. I wanted to smash the principal's face—even if it meant going to jail.

His desk buzzer sounded. He flicked a switch.

"Yes?"

It was the intercom to the receptionist.

"Mr. Masefield."

"Tell him to wait a moment."

Masefield's voice broke in. "It can't wait. That kid has gotten away from us! He's locked himself in an aircar. Who owns that Cad Super?"

I staggered the principal with a straight hard punch in the mouth. I threw another to his jaw and another in his solar plexus. I leaped onto his desk and seized him by the throat and battered his head against the desk top. Then I drove my fist into his face again and again until he lost consciousness.

Celia had had the presence of mind to turn off the microphone. I flicked it on.

"Masefield?" I was trusting the phone to depersonalize my voice.

"Yes."

"The owner will be right out to open it. Is there anyone by the car now?"

"Officer Fegerty."

"Good. Then the boy can't get away. Come to my office for a minute."

I kicked at the control panel and ripped out all the wires in sight, then socked the principal three or four more times for good measure. We exited as casually as we could, nodding pleasantly as we passed Masefield in the hall. Then we broke into a frantic run, through the inner and outer doors, pausing only long enough for Celia to smash the electric eye mechanism with her purse as the outer door swung shut. Nicely competitive of her.

We raced out to the parking lot. The cop was standing beside our car, and I could see Freddie cowering in the back seat, behind closed windows and locked doors.

"Officer Fegerty!" I said breathlessly. "Mr. Masefield says for you to come to the principal's office immediately! Something's happened."

He hesitated. "What about the kid?"

"We'll watch him! You'd better hurry!"

He headed for the administration building at a lumbering trot.

We waved wildly to Freddie. He pounced, with uncontrollable joy, on the door release. Celia plunged into the car, and then I. Out of the corner of my eye I could see that the policeman had stopped. He was viewing us with uncertainty. Then he yelled and started to run toward us, unlimbering his gun from its holster.

My trembling fingers fitted the key into the ignition. I heard a shot and a thudding sound. Then another, and a hole appeared in my side and front windows. I gunned our car like fury and we rocketed into the air so fast that Celia, holding Freddie tightly in her arms, moaned at the terrible acceleration.

We were far above Chicago's islands. Nothing, not even a police car, could catch our Cad Super.

I turned to my son. "You're a bright boy, Freddie. I'm proud of you." A real competitor at heart.

Then my eye caught the great municipal sign, with its motto I WILL COMPETE. And I realized for the first time the seriousness of what we had done.

"The alarm will be out any minute," I told Celia. "I must land."

I nosed our ship down to the lowest air line, merging with slow local traffic above the city. For once I was not pleased to be driving such a conspicuous car. Where to land? Certainly not my usual parking lot. They'd check there as a matter of routine.

Celia read my thoughts. "Where would they least expect us?"

"Navy Pier traffic fines bureau!" I exclaimed. "They have a free parking lot there."

"That's good, for the car," said Celia, "but risky for us." She thought. "The Art Institute. They have a private lot and we're members."

"Ridiculous!" I started to say, then checked myself. "That's good. That's cultural. The cops would never think we'd go looking at pictures."

There would be people there, a crowd in which we could lose ourselves. A big building where we could remain all day, if necessary, without attracting suspicion. A place where I could think. I desperately needed to think.

"I don't want to go to the Art Institute," Freddie whined. "I want to go home."

Celia tried to comfort him. "Mother wants to go home too, dear one, but we can't go home just now."

We sure can't, I thought grimly. I maneuvered past the petal-shaped peak of Tribune Tower with its banner—100% COMPETITION MEANS 100% AMERICAN, past the upper stories of the Prudential Building ("WE'RE COMPETING—ARE YOU?"), past the squat old Bible Federation building (COMPETER, REMEMBER ST. PETER!), and at last settled with a sigh behind the museum.

"I want to go home," Freddie whimpered, his eyes starting to tear again. He was a thin, rather bony little boy, with light brownish eyes like Celia's, and a forceful jaw that was quivering now at the point of a sob.

Celia caressed his curly brown hair. "We're going to spend the entire day together, darling. We're going to look at some wonderful pictures."

I was irritated, but I guess you can't expect too much understanding of a kid.

We entered the building from the rear, parking lot entrance. The Art Institute was one of those wild, non-geometric creations of the Twenty-first century reconstruction period. It was a flat, one-storied building. The outside was partially circular, with a pearly transparent roof. Inside it formed a spiral, with galleries partitioned off like the chambers of nautilus shell. At the eye of the spiral stood a small sunken garden and tea room.

I looked at my watch. Ten-fifteen. "We can stay here until five, if need be," I told Celia. "Don't leave the building until I return."

"Where are you going?" Celia was calm outwardly. Only her eyes registered alarm.

"To see my lawyer. Then to the office. Then to the bank. I have a hunch that ten thousand won't be enough for our present needs."

"Bart, I—"

"Let's not discuss it now. First I want to find out how we stand legally."

I patted Freddie's cheek. "Bye, son. I'll try to get back in time for lunch with you and mother."

I strode off, pausing at the main entrance to call the law offices of Devron, Beach and Feldman. Beach was my man and he was in. I hailed a coptercab and we lumbered over to the gold-black, ellipsoid Richmond Building opposite City Hall.

Beach was a Top Competitor, a slim, trim, fit, fighting individual with graying black hair, and a smiling suntanned face underscored by hard lines of determination. He was humorless, busy and abrupt in all his dealings, but he'd never yet lost a case for me.

"I have to be in court in ten minutes, Bart. Can you give it to me briefly?"

"I don't know if I can. There are so many aspects. To begin with, I assaulted a man. Knocked him unconscious."

"Government official? Top Competitor?"

"No, just a private school principal."

"Injure him badly?"

"I don't know. He was still out when I left."

Beach's eyes flickered with surprise.

"You're not a violent type. He must have provoked you?"

"Called my son non-competitive."

Beach dismissed the matter with a gesture. "You've nothing to worry about." He paused, his shrewd eyes surveying. "Is that all?"

"Unfortunately not." I was ashamed to tell the whole story, and I've told Beach some pretty raw ones in the past without flinching. "In effect, I've defied a court order concerning my son. Obstructed justice, you might say."

"Leave the legal definitions to me," said Beach tersely. "Tell me what you did."

"Well, the principal was turning my son Freddie over to some guy from the Special Training and Re-Education School. Without any advance notice. Just bang! Like that. Called Celia and me in this morning to tell us.

As though it were already an accomplished fact. Well, I knew it was illegal on his part. Imagine that! Taking a kid away from his parents for five years! So I snatched up Freddie and left him with Celia in a safe place and came directly to you. Beach, I want to fight this. I want you to take a law book and beat the city's brains in!"

Beach stood up. He would not look me in the eye, but the hard lines on his face showed up like steel cables.

"I won't touch the case. You'll have to find someone else."

A wave of shock and fear surged through my veins. "Beach, you're the best man in the city! You've got to take it!"

"I couldn't win. No one could. You're in trouble, Bart. You'd better hand over your son to the school." He was thinking out loud. "Plead emotional upset on your part. It's a terrible thing for a father, a Top Competitor, to be told he has a non-competitive son. You momentarily lost control of yourself. Bring him to the school voluntarily. Say you thrashed him within an inch of his life. Say you've been too busy competing to pay much attention to your son's upbringing. But now you're turning him over to the school, and you want them to indoctrinate him thoroughly in the principles of democracy.

"You'd have a scandal, of course, but people would sympathize with you. Applaud your resoluteness.

"Yes, you would get off that way. I still couldn't handle the case, naturally, but I can recommend someone."

"Beach," I said firmly, "I won't give the boy up."

He was silent for a moment. "Then you're ruined. You're a fugitive from justice. Your only hope is in Australia."

That was a slap in the face. "Australia!" I shouted. "That crummy socialist state? That shlub society? No sir, I'm staying right here, in the free competitive world!"

Beach looked ostentatiously at his watch. "You'll have to excuse me. I have a case in court. A murder case, where I can do my client some good."

He picked up his briefcase and went to the door, and stood there courteously showing me out. "I don't imagine I'll be seeing you again, Bart. Take a lawyer's parting advice. Don't go home. Don't go to your office. Put your family on the next ship for Australia." He put his hand on my shoulder, adding, not unkindly, "I also advise you to leave this building quickly. You realize that I must report you to the police."

I free-fell down the elevator shaft, stopping at the mezzanine rather than the ground floor. There was a balcony and staircase overlooking the main entrance. I could see a policeman loitering at the doorway. I had no reason to believe Beach had immediately made his report. Even if he had, was it likely the police could reach the scene sooner than it took me to drop thirty-eight stories? Nevertheless, there the cop was.

I went back to the elevator, rode the updraft to the roof landing. A police ship was idling over the Richmond Building. Coincidence. I saw a taxi drop his fare only twenty feet away, and I wanted desperately to hail the cab, but I couldn't take the chance. I remained for a minute by the doorway. The police ship also lingered.

I asked a building employe where the freight elevator was. He pointed the direction, and I stripped off my suit jacket and folded it around my waist beneath my shirt. Then I rolled up my shirt sleeves and stepped into the down-shaft. I hit bottom two floors below street-level. There was a clerk in a receiving room.

"Has some office furniture come in for 1108?" I asked in a shlub accent.

"Nothin' yet," said the clerk.

I thumbed at the doorway. "That the freight tube?"

"Yup."

"Maybe they're waiting for me outside?"

It was a silly thing to say but it gave me the excuse of looking. I ducked my head out and saw that the dock was empty. There was a rush of sewer-tainted air, and the hum of the city's subterranean conveyer belt.

"The idiots!" I exclaimed for the clerk's benefit. "There they are at the next building."

I slammed the door and hopped onto the belt which was moving at about five miles an hour. I jumped off at the next dock we came to, rode the freight shaft up, then got off at the sixth floor.

Quickly I rolled down my sleeves, whipped out the jacket from under my shirt, smoothed down my hair and was presentable again. I walked around until I found the passenger shaft and descended to the ground level.

I was more angry than frightened. I a fugitive! A Top Competitor forced to flee through the city sewers! What a rotten, unjust turn of events.

What next? I was outside now, on the pedestrian belt moving eastward toward the lake. Obviously, whatever we did, wherever we went, money would be necessary. The bank, then. I would draw out my entire account.

A second thought. No, not the entire amount; that might excite suspicion, cause a spot check with the police. Half would be better—a hundred and twenty-five thousand.

I entered the 1st National and went to a counter to write out a check. A cautioning light suddenly flared in my brain. What if the authorities had called the bank—frozen my assets?

There's only one safe way to find out, I thought. I wrote out a small check to cash—fifty credits. Went to one of the many tellers, handed it through the cage. I knew, of course, that my picture was automatically taken as I did so.

The teller glanced curiously at the check, stamped it, and without hesitation handed me a fifty credit note.

I was elated. The bank had not yet been notified. I returned to the counter and wrote out a check in my own name to one hundred twenty-five thousand credits.

I presented it to another teller.

"Your identification, please?"

I flashed my wrist band.

The teller studied the check minutely. "This is a considerable sum. More than I have at my window. Could you wait for just a moment?" He picked up his phone.

A bank guard tapped me on the shoulder.

"Could you come with me, please."

My impulse was to run. A paralyzer pistol was sheathed in his wrist holster. There was no use.

I followed him to the original teller's window.

"I'm sorry, sir," said the man, "but an estop has been put on this account. You will have to return the fifty credits."

"Certainly," I said, hastily whipping out the fifty. I wanted to dash for the door. Out of the corner of my eye I saw the other teller hang up his phone and look about urgently. He had not yet seen me.

"Here is the invalidated check," said the teller. "I suggest you hold onto it."

"Thank you," I said, restraining my hand from grabbing. "Guard," I said, "there's a teller over there motioning for you." I pointed in the opposite direction from the second teller. "I think it's number 16 there."

He went his way. I went my way, as fast as one can in a bank building without starting a chase. I hurried through the doors, waving frantically for a coptercab. One descended.

"Where to?"

Good question. "Fly me over the islands. I have to kill some time."

We ascended. I could just about read the cabbie's mind. "These damn Competitors! So busy and so loaded they have to spend money to kill time." We wafted towards the lakefront. My own thoughts were swirling chaotically. I felt as though someone had turned off the degravity device just as I was stepping into the elevator shaft. The rug—no, the entire floor itself—had been yanked out from under me. I knew now that I was being pursued systematically. It was not yet noon, not yet two hours since the event. Already the subtle, confident, overpowering resources of the state had been brought to bear, narrowing the avenues of escape, cutting off the criminal's life-line. Yet what had made me an outlaw? Love of offspring?

"Do you want me to just keep circling?" said the cabbie.

I made a quick decision. "Board of Trade Building. I'll show you which entrance when we get there."

My office was located there. Undoubtedly it would be under close watch. Probably Charlie Spacker's was also. But I had to communicate with Charlie. Had to get some money. Had to arrange to get out of the country.

In my mind's eye I could visualize two plainclothesmen seated in the anteroom of the firm of Sponsor & Spacker, trying to appear like clients. I could see another detective or two, armed with photograph and paralyzer, keeping vigilance on the roof landing. A few more watching the ground level entrance.

It was hard for me to believe I was that important to the state, worth a platoon of human blood-hounds. And yet, if the state was doing a thorough job at all, one had to assume they were there, and at our home in Mason City, Iowa, and at my club, and at all the space and air terminals as well. But it did not seem likely to me that a detective would actually be sitting in my private office, at my desk, waiting for me to come in through the window. That was the chance I'd have to take.

We approached the massive Board of Trade Building, which resembled the glued-together pipes of an antique pipe-organ, and I pointed and said to the cabbie,

"See that balcony. Let me off there."

The driver stared back at me, wide-eyed. "We aren't allowed to do that, mister."

"I realize that," I said, handing him a twenty credit note. "But I want to play a joke on a friend."

"All right, buddy," he said, maneuvering his copter closer to the building. "Remember, if you land on the pavement below, I don't offer any guarantees."

He hovered stationary beside my balcony and I leaped across the air space of two or three feet and slipped and clung, and finally scrambled to safety.

I could see into my darkened office. It didn't look as if anyone was there. Then a new problem presented itself. How to open the unbreakable strontium-alloy window? There was no way at all to do it from the outside.

Why hadn't I thought of that!

I looked down sixty-eight stories, and looked up forty-one stories, and realized I was trapped.

Unless I could reach the balcony outside Charlie's office. Oh my God, I thought—a human fly act! That was ten feet away, and I am six-foot-one tall. Moreover, the wind was blowing in the wrong direction. And the face of the building was perfectly smooth. Not a thing to use as a hand-hold.

There was another possibility. I took off one of my shoes and hurled it at Charlie's window. It missed, but fortunately remained on the balcony. I took off the other one. It struck his window with a dull clonk.

If Charlie was out of his office—. Well, I couldn't be any more in a jam without shoes than with shoes.

A face appeared at the window. Our secretary Claire. She peered out for an instant, but the angle was too extreme for her to see me waving crazily. As she disappeared I let out an anguished shout. She reappeared, pressed the window lever, and stuck her head outside.

"Mr. Sponsor!" she said in amazement.

"Is Spacker there?" I had no time to dwell on the situation.

"No, Mr. Sponsor, he's still in the pit." A frown crossed her forehead. "But there are some gentlemen—waiting to see you."

"Yes, I know about them. Now, Claire. Come into my office through the adjoining door and open this window. And first please reach out and get my shoes."

She smiled, and I too had to see the humor.

Claire was a pretty-faced brunette with ultra-fair complexion and a tendency towards overweight which kept her eating prescriptions instead of meals. She couldn't compete with our robot steno, but customers like to deal with a human being. And she was loyal.

She let me in and handed me my shoes.

I sat down, put them on. "Those men outside are not to know I'm here." This was the real test of her loyalty.

Claire nodded tersely. She was not a dumb girl.

"I'm in serious trouble, Claire. The less you know about it the better, but it's all tied up with the crisis on Venus. Were you able to book passage for me?"

"Yes, you've a reservation on the midnight rocket."

"Good! When's your lunch hour?"

"I'm on it now, Mr. Sponsor."

"Will you do me a tremendous favor, Claire? I know it's an imposition, but it's quite urgent. Would you go down to the Venus Spaceship Line and pick up that ticket for me? And while you're at it, get two more tickets on the same ship, but separated from me. Do you understand? Have them bill us as usual."

"Under what name, Mr. Sponsor?" She was a canny girl.

"Leave all three open under our company name." This wasn't much better than 'Mr. & Mrs. Bart Sponsor & Son', but it left us some leeway to juggle identities. Perhaps trade tickets with three shlubs at the last minute. "I hope you don't mind this imposition." I added.

"I'll be very glad to do this for you, Mr. Sponsor." She hesitated. "Do you want me to bring the tickets back to the office? What should I do with them if you've left in the meantime?"

These were knowledgeable questions. How much did she already know? Was Claire really loyal, or was she planning already to tip off the police? Have them trail me, trap Celia and Freddie as well? That was one of those unavoidable risks.

"Mmm. Good question, Claire. Leave them in an envelope at the mail desk of the Conrad-Palmer Hotel ... under my name."

Hell, I thought. If she's going to betray me, the name won't make any difference. Otherwise, I'll need my own name for identification, in order to pick up the envelope.

They had not gotten around to examining my personal files. The drawers were still locked, and my slim, antique missile-gun was still filed under "W" (for weapon). I slipped it into my pocket and began rifling through my papers. I had never, to be truthful, expected to be in a situation as bad as this. But Top Competitors have to be prepared for some rough tactics.

Under "I" was a set of false identity papers. Under "S" was a sleep bomb—strenuously outlawed in private hands. Under "B" were various blackmail letters, including one I secretly held over Spacker. I looked hopefully under "M" for money, but there my foresight had failed me. It had never occurred to me that a man with a quarter of a million in the bank, and three times as much in securities, would some day need money.

I did find something under "M" that made me pause. Mendelsohn. It was a yellowed old folder, certainly the oldest in the entire file. My thoughts suddenly swirled back to college days. This was a project we had worked up together, when Solly was still hot on soil chemistry, and I hadn't settled on anything definite except somehow making a fortune. This was a technique for creating tillable topsoil out of solid rock in ten short years. About a million times faster than nature could do it, but who wanted to wait ten years?

Not I, at least. And when I, who was to do the selling, cooled off on the idea, Solly lost interest too.

Intriguing, though. Maybe Solly would like it back. Maybe the poor shlub could use it on Primus Gladus. I began stuffing things in my briefcase.

Charlie Spacker returned. I could hear him enter the adjoining office. I gave him time to settle down at his desk, then made my appearance.

"Bart!" He was genuinely startled. Charlie was a heavy-set, muscular man with deep resonant voice, short-cut wiry hair, and ruggedly sculptured Roman features. He was a good bargainer by instinct, a rough competitor within established ground rules, but weak on the frontiers, slow to assimilate new ideas, fearful of decisions.

"You've been a long time in returning, Charlie. I've waited here almost an hour. The gentlemen outside are growing impatient."

Charlie was confused. "They know you're here?"

"How do you think I got in? Through the window?"

"But I thought you were in serious trouble. Beach called and said—"

"I know all about that. Beach is behind the time, and he's not getting any more of our business, do you understand?" I had been speaking harshly. Now I fell into the familiar friendly vein. "Charlie, this is the situation. I came within an inch of getting my head chopped off. But I spoke to the Central Committeeman, and the matter's being straightened out."

I paced the office casually. "It's costing me money, of course. A cool half-million."

Charlie's eyes grew to the first magnitude. "Canopus! Have you got that much?"

"Not quite. Not in cash, anyway. There are some securities I can't put on the market right now. So I'm a hundred thousand short. Which isn't so much, actually."

I had to make this sound completely nonchalant. "I thought I'd borrow it from the business for thirty days. I assume that's all right with you?"

Spacker is no fool either. He hesitated. "Well sure, Bart, if we have it. But you know, with this Venus crisis we're running pretty close."

I exploded. "What do you mean, 'if we have it'! Our assets top thirty million."

"You weren't in the pit this morning, Bart. The way Venus commodities are going, we'll be damn lucky to cover our commitments."

"*That* bad? Well, it's a good thing I'm leaving for Venus tonight." I paused. "All right, Charlie, then make me a personal loan."

"I'd be glad to, Bart. But ... considering the circumstances, how can I be sure you'll come back from Venus?" Spacker was shrewd.

"Don't be absurd, Charlie." I tried to make light of his bullseye. "If that bothers you, I'll give you two-for-one in government series R as collateral."

Spacker shook his head. "If something should go wrong with this deal you've made, then the government will be able to reclaim them as forfeit. And I'll be out a hundred thousand."

I was swallowing the humiliation, frustrated with a rage that I had to conceal. I was furious at his lack of trust, and chagrined that he was so well justified.

"All right, Charlie," I said cordially. "I'm a little hurt by your suspiciousness, but you have me at a disadvantage. I need the money. I suppose I could raise it some other way, but then that would delay my departure for Venus. And you know that our mutual welfare is tied up with the trip.

"If so many things worry you about this personal transaction, let me put your mind at ease. I'll sign over my equity in the business as security for the loan. Is that good enough?"

Charlie was now his best competitive self. "Look at it from my point of view, Bart. If you didn't return, the business would become all mine anyway. Isn't that right?" A bland look of innocence spread over his face, a mask concealing the saturnine smile. "Bart, I suggest you delay your trip for a day or so. Raise the money some other way."

I held back long enough to believe my ears. Then I drew my gun. "You bastard!"

"You can't force me to sign! I'd repudiate it by phone the minute you left!"

"I'll kill you!"

"That won't get you the money. You'll rot in the slave-mines of Mercury!"

True. A feeling of fatalism swept over me like ocean surf. I opened Spacker's door and called out to the detectives:

"If you gentlemen will step in here, we've just received word of Mr. Sponsor's whereabouts."

Then I stepped back behind the door jamb, leveling the gun at Spacker. He knew I meant silence. He knew I would kill.

The detectives entered. I jumped behind them. "Raise your hands!"

They complied.

"You too, Spacker. Now, the three of you turn your backs to me and walk to the wall. Keep those hands high!"

I opened my briefcase with one hand, withdrew the sleep bomb, hurled it at their feet. The detectives knew what it was after one gasp, and tried to hold their breath. But one gasp is enough. They crumpled to the floor, unconscious. I closed Spacker's door and hung up the 'Do Not Disturb' sign.

Our robot secretary was taking a flurry of phone messages. I waited patiently in the anteroom till Claire returned.

"Here they are," she said soberly, handing me the envelope. "Three berths on the *Sophocles*."

"That's wonderful, Claire! Thanks a lot. By the way, you'll notice that those gentlemen have left. The matter is all straightened out."

A smile wreathed her face. "I'm very happy for you, Mr. Sponsor."

"In celebration, you know what we're going to do? We're going to give you the rest of the day off!"

She was enthralled. I waited until five minutes after she'd left, then walked briskly to the down-shaft.

I had to assume there were detectives posted at the main floor entrance. And on the roof. And even perhaps in the freight entrance. I got off on the second floor.

I walked down the corridor, studying the signs on doorways. There was a market research firm, Mechlen Drew Inc., that occupied a large suite, with several labeled doors. I opened one that said 'Employes' and found myself in a room with a medium-sized computer and several preoccupied mathematicians.

I went directly and purposefully to the window, opened it, and calculated the distance to ground level. Twelve feet maybe. The employes looked at me with faint interest. Someone from the building maintenance department, probably.

For a minute or two I watched the pedestrians glide by on the conveyer belt. I saw no evidence of the police.

"I think I'll have to examine this from the outside," I said to the employes. "Will one of you close the window after me?"

I got out on the sill, eased my body down, hung by my fingertips for a moment, then let go. I could see a puzzled expression at the window as I glided away and became lost in pedestrian cross-traffic.

In a mood of self-congratulation, I headed for the Art Institute. The mood vanished as I passed the first newsstand. Boldly on its display screen was a front page story about the fugitive Sponsor family. There were pictures, of course. They didn't have a very good one of Celia. College graduation shot. She had nothing to worry about. The photo of Freddie was better, but the city is full of skinny seven-year-olds with sensitive features. No great risk of recognition there.

But the one of me! A perfect likeness. Repeated on an endless number of newsstands between the Board of Trade Building and the museum. The large, oval-shaped bald head, shorn of all but a trace of sideburns. The straight, prominent nose with flaring nostrils. The large, sensual lips. The hard-clamped jaw.

Thanking Zeus for Chicago's anonymous millions, I entered the quietly thronged Art Institute.

Celia and Freddie were looking at paintings of the Prismatic school, without much enthusiasm, when I found them. Their greeting made me feel like a hero.

"Daddy!" said Freddie, hitting my leg joyfully as Celia embraced me with a passionate kiss.

"It's one-thirty," said Celia softly, achingly. "We were so worried."

"Let's go eat," I suggested, suddenly aware of hunger pangs.

"We already have, but it'll be much nicer this time."

We went to the tea room. Alongside was the sunken garden, with its dwarf trees and moist green grass and bubbling waterfall. Three or four pieces of ancient sculpture—smooth white marble of the Greeks—stood in the garden on pedestals. Somehow these had survived the destruction.

"Nothing else remained of the whole collection," said Celia sadly. "Renoirs, Rembrandts, Raphaels—all, all gone."

"I'm tired, mommy. Why can't we go home now?"

"After a while, dear. Poor kid! He's weary of looking at pictures, and so am I."

"Freddie," I asked, "why didn't you like to play games with the other children at school?" Celia glanced at me disapprovingly.

"Oh, I like to play games. But ... it just seems that when everyone's trying so hard to win ... it spoils the fun. You know."

"Leave him alone, Bart."

I finished my ersatz soup and my synthetic sandwich, and drank down a cup of chemical coffee, and felt much better.

Freddie napped on one of the garden benches, and that was a good thing for him and for us. We had to talk, weigh alternatives, make plans.

"The real crisis," I said, "is at five o'clock when this place closes. Then we have to get into our ship and fly somewhere. Wherever we go there'll be police looking for a green Cad Super with Iowa license plates."

"We have one advantage at that time," said Celia. "Rush hour. If you can stay in the thick of traffic ... and not hedge-hop."

"Don't worry!"

"The real crisis, I think, is when we board the Venus ship," said Celia. "The police will be watching all departures, checking identities, just as a matter of routine."

"That's true, but we don't go aboard as a threesome. You and Freddie earlier. And I at the last minute, with false identity papers."

Celia shook her head as if warding off an unpleasant thought. "Aren't you afraid that when Spacker wakes up he'll tell them about the Venus ship?"

"According to my information, the sleep bomb knocks you out for ten or eleven hours. A doctor can bring you out of it a little sooner, but you still don't regain your full senses right away."

"Even allowing ten hours, Bart. One and ten is eleven. Our ship leaves at twelve o'clock. That means we face one hour of supreme risk."

She was right, of course. And there was one more source of anxiety that I thought it best not to mention. Claire. What would Claire say if she found out about the sleep bomb? If she went back to the office for any reason this afternoon? Or if the police found out in some manner? Surely they would go looking for the detectives. Surely they would question Claire. What would she tell them?

Five o'clock. Exit separately through the rear door to the parking lot.

First Celia, walking briskly, with keys to the car in her gloved hand. Unaware how I stare at her handsome figure, voluptuous movements of hip and thigh. How akin the awareness of danger and awareness of sex!

She opens the car door, turns the ignition key, idles the engine.

Next, Freddie, as well coached as possible. Unhurried, lackadaisical. Taking a slow, wandering path, oblivious of the peril, curious about the other cars, taking his time.

He reaches our car and Celia scoops him up, and I see him clamber over the front seat and bury himself in the back.

Then I, striding heavily, hastily. Briefcase in hand. Looking neither right nor left. Lowering chin almost onto chest. Waiting for a voice behind me. Expecting a shout: 'Wait! Stop!'

I reach our car, jump in, slam the door, open the throttle. We ascend. Circle into the lowest, slowest, most congested local traffic lane, westward bound over Chicago.

I didn't much like Celia's suggestion. But I couldn't think of a better one. And we had to spend the next five or six hours somewhere.

"So why not the Mendelsohns?" said Celia. "It's a little early for their party, but I'm sure we'll be welcome."

"All right. But we've got to keep quiet about our ... troubles. I don't want that shlub to have the last laugh on me."

It was an evening in early fall, and the sun was setting, but not fast enough for my comfort. I craved the protection of darkness. We already had passed two police cars headed eastward, and each time I cringed helplessly, and Celia and Freddie ducked down out of sight. Possibly the red sunset tones were falsifying the green of our car. Otherwise, I can't see how they overlooked us.

Traffic was starting to thin out as we arrived over the Mendota district of Chicago. This was kind of a marginal area—no longer desirable, not yet slum—where respectable poor people maintained some semblance of pride in their old dilapidated solar-heated homes. It was an area so thick with grime and industrial soot, that I had a hard time making out the roof markers from two-hundred feet. The glass and concrete dwellings were universally alike in pattern, a hollow square with patio in the center. Yet despite the general poverty below, I failed to see a single house that didn't have a rattletrap aircar of some kind parked in the rear. All except the Mendelsohn house. The Mendelsohns never owned a car. They had turned their backyard into a vegetable garden.

"Think they'll mind if I land there?"

"Not when they're leaving tomorrow."

I landed gently, nevertheless. Solly was sensitive about plants.

I think they were really astonished to see us. The girls ran into each other's embrace with squeals of recognition. Solly and I shook hands with a good deal more restraint. Dolores was tossling Freddie's hair. Then we went into their house.

It was pretty bare, of course. They had packed most of their things; probably had them stored aboard ship by now. But there was enough furniture left that went with the house for us to sit down on.

"How wonderful! How wonderful of you to come and see us!" said Dolores. She was a tall, dark, big breasted girl with classical features in the Byzantine sense. Her hair was black, her movements languid, her voice deep and melodius.

"We couldn't see you go to the stars without saying goodbye," said Celia.

"We talked about you so often," Dolly said. "Wondering how you were. What you were doing."

I found it hard to imagine this exotic, beautiful woman transplanted to an alien world in the role of pioneer farmgirl.

"We've thought about you too," said Celia. "So many times."

It was awkward. Solly and I hadn't exchanged more than five words.

"Would you like some refreshments?" said Dolly. "Drinks? Something to eat?" She smiled at me and smiled at Freddie, and nodded yes until Freddie nodded with her.

"Sure you do," she said.

We laughed. Dolly stood up. "We weren't expecting our guests for another hour, but everything's ready."

She and Celia and Freddie went into the kitchen.

I hated to be left alone with Solly, and I suppose the feeling was reciprocal.

"Are you glad to be going?" I inquired neutrally.

"Very."

"How long does it take to get there?"

"Two and a half years."

"That's a long time!"

"Not considering the distance. Primus Gladus is nine-tenths of a light-year away."

"Funny," I said, "a star being that close, undiscovered until this century."

"It's not a bright star. Half the luminosity of our sun. For all we know, there may be others just as close." Solly meditated on the idea.

"I suppose that's possible," I said. "Must be thousands of stars in the southern skies—faint stars, I mean—that haven't been measured."

We were both silent. There seemed nothing further to say. The distance was as far between us as between Sol and Primus Gladus. I fumbled in my briefcase.

"This is something that may interest you, Solly." I handed him the folder containing his topsoil project. "Found it in my file just this afternoon. Thought maybe you could use it where you're going."

He looked at it. His forehead wrinkled in a frown.

"Remember?" I cued him. "College days?"

A light came into his eyes from a source thousands of light-years away. "Oh yes," he uttered slowly, a faint smile touching the corners of his mouth. "That was our big business venture. The Topsoil Initiator." He looked at me peculiarly. "Bart, how come you kept it all these years?"

"I always thought it was a good idea." This was not a lie. "But why," I said, "haven't *you* done anything with it?"

"O-o-o-oh," he drawled, "no drive, I guess. The real reason, I guess, is that I never had enough money to buy a barren, rocky acre where I could give it a practical tryout."

"Ten years seems like such a long time to wait for results," I said.

Solly reflected with that faint remembering smile on his lips. "It did then."

The girls returned with food and drink, and somehow Solly and I had warmed up over the topsoil recollection, and we all became quite gay and animated and loud-talking, and I suppose it was a little like old times.

Then a little while later Celia took her purse in the other room, and when she came out she handed Dolores an envelope.

I knew what was in it, and I wanted to shout, 'My God, don't do it! That's all the money we have in the world!' But I couldn't get the words out, and Celia said:

"Dolly, here is something for you from us. It's a going-away present. We want you to have it before the others come."

"How nice," said Dolly. "What can it be?"

She opened the envelope, and a mixed expression played across her face—delight and dismay.

"Why, it's money!... A lot of money!... Thousands!"

She turned her head away in reluctance, then handed back the envelope.

"Oh, no, Celia. We couldn't accept it."

Celia refused to take it back. "Oh now, Dolly," she snapped, "don't be stuffy and proud and stupid! We have millions. We *want* you to have it. You certainly need it; you can't deny that. So please accept it and make us happy."

"It's wonderful of you both," said Solly. "But you know how it is. We just can't."

"We just can't," repeated Dolly.

"Oh please, please," cried Celia, and she was really getting emotional. "Don't you realize. This is the last time we'll ever see you! You're going to a far-away world, our two dearest friends. And this may seem like a lot of money, but it really isn't. It's all the gifts and presents we would give you in a lifetime, rolled up into one. It's funny little baby clothes when your children are born. It's anniversary gifts. It's for your boy's bar mitzvah and your daughter's confirmation. It's wedding presents when they grow up. It's—it's funeral wreaths!"

Celia started to cry, and Dolly started to cry, and they hugged each other and started to cry even more, and the tears rolled down their cheeks. And the tears rolled down my cheeks, and Solly's too, I guess, and we shook hands very solemnly. And Celia stuffed the envelope into Dolly's hand. And then all of us really cut loose and bawled—I covering my face with my hands, and Solly burying his face in a handkerchief. Only Freddie wasn't crying at first. He was just standing there looking bewildered. And then he got scared and started to cry too, hanging onto my pants leg with one hand, and trying to reach Celia with the other.

And then, thank God, the first guests arrived, ringing the bell, so that we had a compelling reason to stop.

The party was still going strong when we left at eleven. Solly and Dolly walked us out to our car. There really wasn't much left to say. We had found each other in friendship again, and would never again be nearer than nine-tenths of a light-year.

"A pity!" said Solly, and I knew what he meant.

The evening was very cool. Celia began to shiver. We took off, and the cabin heater warmed up the thermometer, but still we felt cold. Freddie sat in the front seat between us, dozing lightly.

Our Cad Super roared through the night. Even at full power, Spaceport, Nevada, was thirty minutes away. The moon set rapidly. The night grew darker.

"I fear that we will be caught," said Celia tonelessly, like a voice dissociated from body.

Our ship's nose wavered slowly between Procyon and Pollux, Canis Minor and Gemini, back and forth, droning on in the blackness.

"I fear for our little boy," said Celia like a soul lost in a maze of warped space. "What will they do to him?"

"They'll never lay hands on him," I said softly.

The Serpent writhed and Charioteer rocked as Twins dueled the Crab and Hunter pursued Bull.

"That was a fine gesture you made," Celia whispered.

"What?"

"Giving them the money. I'm proud of you."

The lights of Spaceport glowed on the horizon. It was a vast complex of launching sites, covering a hundred square miles. But only one ship could blast off at a time, and that ship would be flooded by searchlights. I singled out the Venus rocket and we descended.

It was eleven-thirty-two. I handed Celia her two tickets.

As we approached the Venus compound I could see several police cars parked on the field. Passengers seemed to be leaving rather than entering the ship. The gangway was crowded with people pouring out of the spacelock.

"They're looking for us," I muttered.

"Is that why they're all getting off?" said Celia.

"They must be shaking down the entire ship."

"This is the moment I feared." She tightened her grip on Freddie.

"There must be a way of getting aboard!" I said.

We edged forward to the gates of the field.

"There is no way of getting aboard," said Celia. Her voice was hopeless. She motioned at a large bulletin board.

The sign read: VENUS FLIGHTS CANCELLED UNTIL FURTHER NOTICE BECAUSE OF CIVIL DISORDERS ON THAT PLANET.

I was weary and defeated, but I said, "Honey, we're not licked. We can still go to Australia."

"I have a better idea," Celia exclaimed. It was as though a new current of life, a new gusher of hope, had burst through the surface. "Let's go to Primus Gladus!"

It was four in the morning. We had told Solly and Dolly the straight story.

"Do you think we can get a berth on the ship?" my wife queried anxiously. "Is there any way you can help us?"

The Mendelsohns exchanged glances.

"I don't know," said Solly. "Truthfully. Let me think about it a few minutes."

"Since you've told us the truth about yourselves," said Dolly, "do you mind hearing some things you don't know about us?"

"All cards might as well be face up," I replied.

"Well listen, you two. It isn't easy to emigrate to another system. If you're a shlub, yes. But not if you're a soil chemist, or any other kind of scientist or advanced technician. Earth won't let the boys with know-how get out of its clutches." Dolly's eyes were burning with a message she only half-dared to communicate. "Does this give you any clues?" she asked, eagerly scanning our faces.

Suddenly the parts fit perfectly. "Solly! You did it deliberately. You washed out of school! You let your career fall to pieces. On purpose!"

Solly was nodding and smiling rather grimly.

"But why?" I demanded. "You had such brilliant prospects here on Earth. Why did you do it?"

"Surely you of all people must know by now," said Dolly excitedly. "Can you and your family go on living in this kind of a world? Can you endure this police-state tyranny now that you know what it is? Can you accept the hypocrisy, the masquerade behind pious slogans? What is this thing they call Competition? Is it really good? Is it really the expression of democracy? Is it what they want or is it forced on them?"

"Dolly, you're asking more questions than you're answering," said Celia, trying to head her off.

"Or is it organized greed? Simple dog-eat-dog? The law of jungle cunning and brute force re-affirmed? If we must compete, let it not be as maggots swarming over a half-eaten pie! Let's get people to vie with one another in service to mankind!"

Dolly had worked herself into a kind of evangelical zeal, with Solly nodding hypnotically in agreement.

I answered calmly, trying not to strain our newly healed friendship. "I don't go along with you on some of the things you say, Dolly. I personally think competition is the mainspring of progress—"

Solly started to protest.

"—material progress," I added.

"Well, maybe," said Celia, and in a flash I could see what had gone wrong with Freddie's home-life, from the school principal's point of view. "But I can't see what competitiveness has to do with creative art, or the pure sciences, or philosophy. I think it's positively destructive in those areas. The real struggle there is internal, not external. To me, competition is only a part of life not the whole of it."

"You're all wrong!" I shouted. "My only concern is with the welfare of Freddie. That's what got us into this predicament. I want you to understand that I'm for the system ninety-five per cent!"

Solly, Dolly, and Celia smiled. That irritated me but I let the matter drop.

"Let's consider what's to be done," I said.

"Yes," said Solly very seriously. "I can tell you this about the star-ship. On a voyage of two and a half years, nothing can be done haphazardly, at the last minute. Every berth has to be accounted for long in advance. Our baggage has been calculated down to the last ounce. The number of farming implements, the number of livestock—even the number of children you may have en route!—are strictly allocated."

"In other words, the only way we can get aboard is if someone dies or doesn't show up at the last minute?" said Celia.

"Or if you can persuade someone not to make the trip."

"And in addition get by the police," I added softly.

At seven that morning the airbus stopped to pick up the Mendelsohns and their hand luggage. We had worked out some kind of half-baked plan that I didn't think would go over with the ship's officials. We set a rendezvous time and place and waved them off. Then we got into our Cad Super. For the second time it bore us west to Spaceport.

As we neared the field, Celia commented, "You know, darling, this car is pretty conspicuous in the daytime."

"I'm hungry, mommy," said Freddie who had missed out on breakfast altogether. Celia gave him a soggy hors d'oeuvre, which was all that was left from the Mendelsohn's party.

I had been thinking about what to do with our expensive car. I brought it down almost a mile from the star-ship *Pericles*.

"You two will have to walk the rest of the way," I said cheerily. "I'll meet you at our rendezvous point in about twenty-five minutes."

The time was now seven-thirty. The ship blasted off at nine. I put our car in a steep climb and circled the field at an altitude of ten thousand feet, where I could see which of the many spaceships were loading passengers.

I chose one ship arbitrarily at the opposite end of the field from the star-ship. It turned out to be an Asteroid surveyor, paying its way with a hundred or so passengers to Ganymede. I set down in the adjoining lot, and fixed the degravity controls so that the ship hovered a few inches off the ground, and left it that way to drift across the field with the wind until it attracted the inevitable attention.

I walked to the next shuttle bus stop and rode across to the *Pericles*. It was a gigantic ship, twenty times the capacity of a Venus or Mars rocket. Comet-shaped, engineered to approach fifty per cent of the speed of light through cumulative acceleration, the star-ship had two vast cargo entrances in addition to the passenger airlock. In one, which was now closing, I caught sight of crated farm machinery. Into the other, herds of cattle were being driven.

It was nearly eight o'clock. I approached the *Pericles* warily. We were all supposed to meet by the livestock gate. Dozens of people were milling about, some ranchers, some colonizers, bargaining at the last minute over a sheep or a goat or a horse or a cow to replace a dead or sick animal. That some of the men were detectives I did not doubt. I saw Celia close to the entrance with Freddie. We exchanged glances of recognition, but kept widely separated.

Solly came up. "I checked with the captain about Dolly and me waiving our right to have a child during the voyage, and taking Freddie with us instead. You were right. He wouldn't buy it."

"That was tremendously generous of you even to offer."

"But," said Solly, "there's been one cancellation!"

Our eyes met. "What's the fare?" I inquired.

"Two thousand." Solly looked down for a moment, then threw back his head. "Look, that's still your money, even if you did give it to us. Dolly and I are willing ... would be happy to pay Freddie's fare. And take care of him as our own if you and Celia can't get on."

"My son has no future on Earth," I said. "If Celia's willing, I am. Go talk to her."

Solly went to Celia. She did not once look in my direction and I was glad. In the end, Freddie went with Solly, and I could tell what the lie was. Solly was going to show Freddie the insides of the wonderful ship.

It was a quarter after eight. Only forty-five minutes before take-off. Celia and I were going to be left behind. There didn't seem much reason for further pretense. I took my wife's hand.

"Little did we know how important your going-away present would be. Solly used two thousand of it to pay Freddie's fare."

Celia shook her head. "He didn't have to do that."

"Sweetheart, all we have left is about a hundred and fifty credits."

"That may be all *you* have left," she said proudly, "but that isn't all *we* have left. If my addition is correct, we have ninety thousand cash credits in my purse, right at this minute!"

"What! How do you mean?"

Celia put her arm in mine. "I played a dirty trick on you, darling. You signed and I added another zero."

"You took out a hundred thousand! No wonder that teller made such a fuss."

"Dear, I thought you might have to use a little bribery. I knew Freddie was in trouble, and that was my fault, of course. I'm the villain in his home-life!" She smiled ruefully, then looked at the *Pericles*, her eyes brimming with tears. "But I had no idea they'd try to take him away from us!"

My thoughts pulsed wildly. "Look, Celia! We can both get aboard! Give me the money!" I took her purse and ran over to the huddle of colonizers.

"I've got ninety-thousand cash credits! Who'll give up his place on the *Pericles*?"

The group turned to face me in astonishment. One man came forward. I thought I saw a gun hidden in his sleeve. "Ninety thousand?"

"That's right. Who wants it?"

"Ninety thousand is a small fortune," said the man. "Anyone with that kind of money shouldn't need to pull up stakes on Earth and start life all over again on a new planet. Should he?"

"I don't imagine so. Who'll take ninety thousand for his place on the *Pericles*?" I repeated over his shoulder.

"Unless he has some special, very compelling reason for leaving Earth," the stranger continued.

A colonizer ran up breathlessly. "Ninety thousand? Let me see it!"

I opened the purse, pulled out the wad of bills, and flung the purse on the ground.

The colonizer riffed through the wad. "That's for me! I'll take it!"

He reached for the money.

"Just a minute," I said. "It's yours after you give that lady over there your berth and make it legal with the ship."

"Hey," said a companion, "how about all your belongings? Your cattle and equipment? You haven't time any more to take it off."

"Heck, my whole outfit isn't worth more than fifteen thousand! I'll give it to the lady."

He ran to Celia and the two of them dashed for the passenger ramp. It was eight-thirty-five. Twenty-five minutes before take-off.

I put the money in my coat pocket.

"I don't think," said the stranger, "that this transaction is going through." He stepped so close we were almost jaw to jaw. "Let me see your identity tag."

"Who are you trying to impersonate?" I said.

"A common ordinary rancher," he replied, flashing his badge. "Now let's see your identification."

"Certainly." I showed him my false wrist tag.

"Donald Simpson, I see." He stared at me through narrowed eyes. "Where did you find that, Mr. Sponsor?"

"Sponsor? Is that the guy you're looking for? I have about a dozen other documents to prove I'm Simpson. If you have the patience to look at them."

I opened the briefcase and handed him the packet. They had cost me thousands and they were awfully good forgeries. They slowed the detective down quite a bit.

"Why are you offering that kind of money to get the lady on board?"

"Because I'm awfully anxious to get rid of her."

"You didn't happen to put a kid aboard that ship too, for the same reason?"

"If you think I did, why don't you go look?"

"I may do that, mister. You know, we can hold this ship on the field for an hour or more if we think it would prove profitable."

I saw Celia waving from the passenger gangway, and the colonizer come sprinting our way.

"It's done!" he exclaimed breathlessly. "Let's have the money."

I reached into my pocket.

The detective laid his hand on my arm. "I said I didn't think this transaction was going through." He turned to the colonizer. "You'd better switch things back to the way they were."

"No," I said, pressing the gun through my coat pocket into the belly of the detective, "don't pay any attention to this character." I crossed over with my other hand and withdrew the money.

"Take this," I said to the colonizer, "and get out of here. Fast as you can!"

He was confused but not on basic things. He took his money and virtually ran.

Ten minutes to nine.

They were closing up the passenger airlock, removing the ramp.

"You know," said the detective very quietly, "my buddy is coming. He won't understand this embrace we're in. I'm quite sure he won't like it one bit."

The last of the animals were being led into the livestock hold. The ranchers were dispersing. The colonizers were all aboard. We stood virtually alone beside the ship.

"I am prepared to be killed," I said, "and to take you with me in the process."

A police car hovered in the air beside us.

"Say!" yelled its pilot. "They've found the Sponsor car over next to the Asteroid surveyor!" He pointed across the field. "They're searching the ship. We've got to help. Hop on!"

I stepped back, with my hand still in my pocket.

"Yes," I said, "hop on!"

The detective clambered aboard the police car. He gave me a look that I'll always remember. A sort of sneer and a sort of smile. "Good luck, Simpson," he said.

The police car whisked away.

Five minutes to nine.

I wheeled and ran to the livestock hold. The hatch was about shut and I knew it was too late. 'Goodbye, my darlings! Goodbye!'

Then the hatch jammed and could not close the last six inches and I saw the reason. A steer had broken loose and charged the door. His head was caught in the opening. His neck had snapped instantly and he was dead.

They re-opened the hatch long enough to fling the thousand-pound carcass onto the field. And that was all the time I needed to come aboard.

A crew member hollered at me: "Do you belong here?"

"Yes," I replied, "I certainly do."

As I said it, the ship blasted heavenward and I was flung to the deck. I started to curse, and then I chuckled. I was stretched out ignominiously beside a cow in the fresh-smelling hay.

I, Bart Sponsor, Top Competitor, starting a new life. This way!

Well Solly, I mused, *understand the planet we're going to has lots of rocky acres.*